Anxiety

What is it and how can I deal with it?

Author: **Sally Wileman**
Illustrator: **Amelia Lee**

Explaining anxiety, fight and flight to children 7 to 12 years old

First published in 2022

ISBN 978-1-7392068-0-2

Text copyright © Sally Wileman

Illustrations copyright © Amelia Lee

The moral right of Sally Wileman to be identified as author of this work has been asserted in accordance with the Copyright, Designs and Patents Act 1988.

All rights reserved.

Typesetting and cover design by The Book Typesetters
www.thebooktypesetters.com

Contents

What happens to our body when the alarm system goes off?	11
Deep breathing	13
5 finger deep breathing	15
Anxiety is like a thermometer	17
Anxiety makes us want to avoid doing things	19
What do I mean when I say let's put anxiety in its place?	21
What else can help? Talking.	23
Mindfulness	25
Bedtime	27
What sets off the fight and flight alarm? A thought	29
Being in scanning mode	31
Don't be like an ostrich and bury your head in the sand	33
Catastrophising	35
Checking, counting and washing	37
Panic	39
Unwelcome thoughts	41
The importance of exercise	43
What does God say about anxiety?	45
Technology	47
Little by little...gradually	49
So what about the fight...the anger?	51
More about anger	53
And finally...Freeze	55
Appendix	59
Looking after our mind	61
About this book	71
About the author	73
Index	75

Hello, my name is Skye and I get worried a lot. A grown-up word for worry is anxiety, and other words for being very worried are fear, frightened, afraid or scared. We sometimes talk about being nervous. So now you know what I'm talking about, I want to let you know how I've learned to put worry in its place. I've learned to beat, defeat, conquer and triumph over anxiety or worry. Worry can make us feel unwell and that we can't do things, but once we know where worry comes from and what it's for, we can take back the power and put it in its proper place.

This is me dressed as a cave person from thousands of years ago. Cave people couldn't talk in the complicated way that we can, and there were many dangers for them, like sabre-toothed tigers. Their brain was more simple than ours, and it reacted to any dangers like an alarm system. We have the same alarm system.

The brain tells the body there's a danger and that the body needs to get ready to deal with the danger. It tells the body to release adrenaline (a hormone) into our blood stream. This makes our heart beat faster so that we can either fight the danger or run away from the danger; that's the flight bit. It's called the fight and flight reaction. The fight is us getting angry, and the flight is us getting anxious because of a supposed threat or danger.

We'll just concentrate on the **flight**...the anxiety...first. We don't have any sabre-toothed tigers anymore and we're not cave people, but our brain and body still react to any dangers, or what our brain thinks are dangers or threats. For example, if I have a spelling test and I haven't practised my spellings, I might think, "Help, I've not practised. I'm not going to do very well. I don't want to do the test." I might feel like running away (flight) from doing the test. Anxiety makes us want to avoid things or run away, but there are things we can do to help us face up to the anxiety, have a go and do what we need to do. We need to put anxiety in its place and show it who is boss!

What happens to our body when the alarm system goes off?

The adrenaline makes our heart beat faster and we might get any of the symptoms in the picture. It's the brain's way of telling the body to get ready to deal with a danger or threat. It happens even when there isn't a serious danger or threat. Going to the dentist, worrying what other children think, reading in front of our class, doing something we've never done before....these can all cause the brain to tell the body that it needs to get ready for flight (run away).

Deep breathing

Let's think about what we can do to calm ourselves down once we start to feel that the alarm is going to go off or it has already gone off.

I'm going to give you the biggest tip to put anxiety in its place...it's...deep breathing...which relaxes us and makes us feel calm again.

5 finger deep breathing

Practise making your breath out, take as long as possible, and then your breath in will be deeper and will make you feel more relaxed. You are breathing in air which is mostly oxygen, and this calms your body. It's like a free medicine that nature has given us. Look at your tummy as you breathe. Let it relax and blow up like a balloon when you breathe in.

Do at least 5 deep breaths. You can use your 5 fingers on one hand to help you count. When you have breathed in, hold the breath for 3 seconds before you do a big, strong blow out as though you're blowing out birthday candles on a cake.

Now make your whole body go heavy like a floppy teddy bear. You are ready to beat anxiety and put it in its place!

Anxiety is like a thermometer

Anxiety might get bad and go up to the top of the anxiety thermometer, but it will always come down when you have done what you need to do: that could be going to school to do a test you are worried about, going to a hospital appointment, or something else. Remember you can deep breathe to make the anxiety go down more quickly. You can look forward to that amazing feeling of being proud of yourself when you have completed the thing you were worried about! Well done!

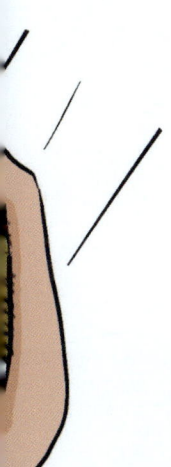

Anxiety makes us want to avoid doing things

We have an urge to run away from things that cause us anxiety, but the more we are brave and do the things that cause us anxiety, the easier things get and one day we won't feel too anxious at all. For example, if you hate reading in front of your class because it makes you really worried and your legs shake, but you decide to be brave and read instead of avoiding it, you will discover that it gets easier each time you do it, until one day you ask to read because you've started to enjoy reading out loud.

What do I mean when I say let's put anxiety in its place?

Well...anxiety is there to keep us safe: to stop us from stepping out onto a busy road and to prevent us from getting too close to the edge of a cliff or lake. It is also useful for making sure that we practise our spellings and for giving us the energy to run a race. Sometimes the alarm goes off when there isn't a real danger. For example, we might have practised our spellings but we're still worried about doing the test because we think we might not do very well. Our heart beats faster, we feel sick, we have sweaty hands and we feel like running away or trying to get out of doing the test. Doing our special, deep breathing is going to calm us down, put anxiety in its place and allow us to do the best we can in the test.

What else can help? Talking.

Talking to a trusted adult, telling them what you're worried about, and making a plan together will help you achieve whatever you need to do. Once you've got a plan, you can relax and trust in the plan.

Remember, anxiety symptoms can be very strong and make you feel poorly and unable to do what you need to do. You are stronger than you think-you can withstand the worry and win!

Talk to yourself in a positive way-reminding yourself that you have the ability to control anxiety; it isn't more powerful than you! Put anxiety in its place. If negative thoughts creep in, change them into positives. Say, "I **can** do what I need to do!"

Mindfulness

Sit in nature and listen to the sounds. Look at the grass, trees, leaves, birds, insects and flowers in as much detail as you can. Focus entirely on nature and you'll be amazed at how relaxed you feel.

Bedtime

Learn to relax for a few minutes everyday and especially at bed time. Tighten all your muscles from top to toe. Start by screwing up your face, then tense your shoulders, arms, hands, chest and tummy muscles, bottom, legs and toes. Let each muscle relax and go heavy so you feel like a floppy teddy bear. Take 5 deep breaths to help yourself relax even more. Listen to some calming music or a bedtime story.

You could make a play list of happy, calming music. Include bird song, whale song and pattering rain or lapping water.

At the back of this book, there is a pretend 'journey' that you could go on as you settle down for bed. Ask an adult to read it to you, to help you relax at bedtime. It really helps me to calm down and relax all my muscles. I hope that it helps you too.

What sets off the fight and flight alarm? A thought

A simple negative thought can trigger the fight and flight reaction, and this leads to us getting a feeling (maybe anxiety or anger) with symptoms such as our heart beating faster.

The feeling affects our behaviour. Look at the example in the picture and see how anxiety affects our behaviour.

We need to break the cycle by being brave, doing the five finger deep breathing exercise and talking positively to ourself saying, "I can do this! I'm going to be brave. I'll feel the symptoms and do it anyway. I'm not afraid of ____ and I'm not afraid of anxiety!" You'll feel so proud of yourself when you've faced your fears and won.

Being in scanning mode

When we get anxious a lot, we tend to get into scanning mode. We're constantly on the lookout for danger and this makes it more likely that the alarm will be activated. It's like we've got antennae on our heads and we're looking out for, and listening out for, 'danger'. What can we do about this?

I tell myself, "Put your worry antennae away Skye! You're safe! There's no real danger! It's your imagination playing tricks on you! Relax, deep breathe and keep calm."

Don't be like an ostrich and bury your head in the sand

Sometimes we don't own up to how we are feeling and we hope that it will just go away. It's important to tell an adult we trust how we're feeling, and ask for help. They'll help us to prepare ourselves by making a plan of the best way to deal with a situation. When we tell someone what we're worried about, it is a huge relief. Sharing a problem makes us feel better. Go ahead, give it a try!

Catastrophising

Sometimes, our imagination and anxiety get together and make up something very frightening. We think the worst is going to happen. I do this a lot, but it's not helpful and anxiety needs putting in its place more than ever. I need to get very good at talking to myself in a positive way and putting anxiety back in its place.

Checking, counting and washing

Sometimes anxiety makes us want to check things more than once or to do some kind of counting and sometimes we want to wash our hands too often, making them sore. Do you do anything more than once because of anxiety? Don't give anxiety the chance to tell you what to do because once is enough! Sometimes we feel like we have to do something like counting or checking, to stop something bad from happening. Anxiety is tricking us into doing these things which don't help us. Doing some deep breaths will help anxiety go back to zero more quickly. Counting and checking make us feel more anxious and they don't help. Ask your family to help you stop counting or checking by distracting you with something fun. A distraction is something that stops you from thinking about whatever you're worrying about and it keeps your mind busy. What about colouring, drawing, playing a game, arts and crafts, watching a film or something else?

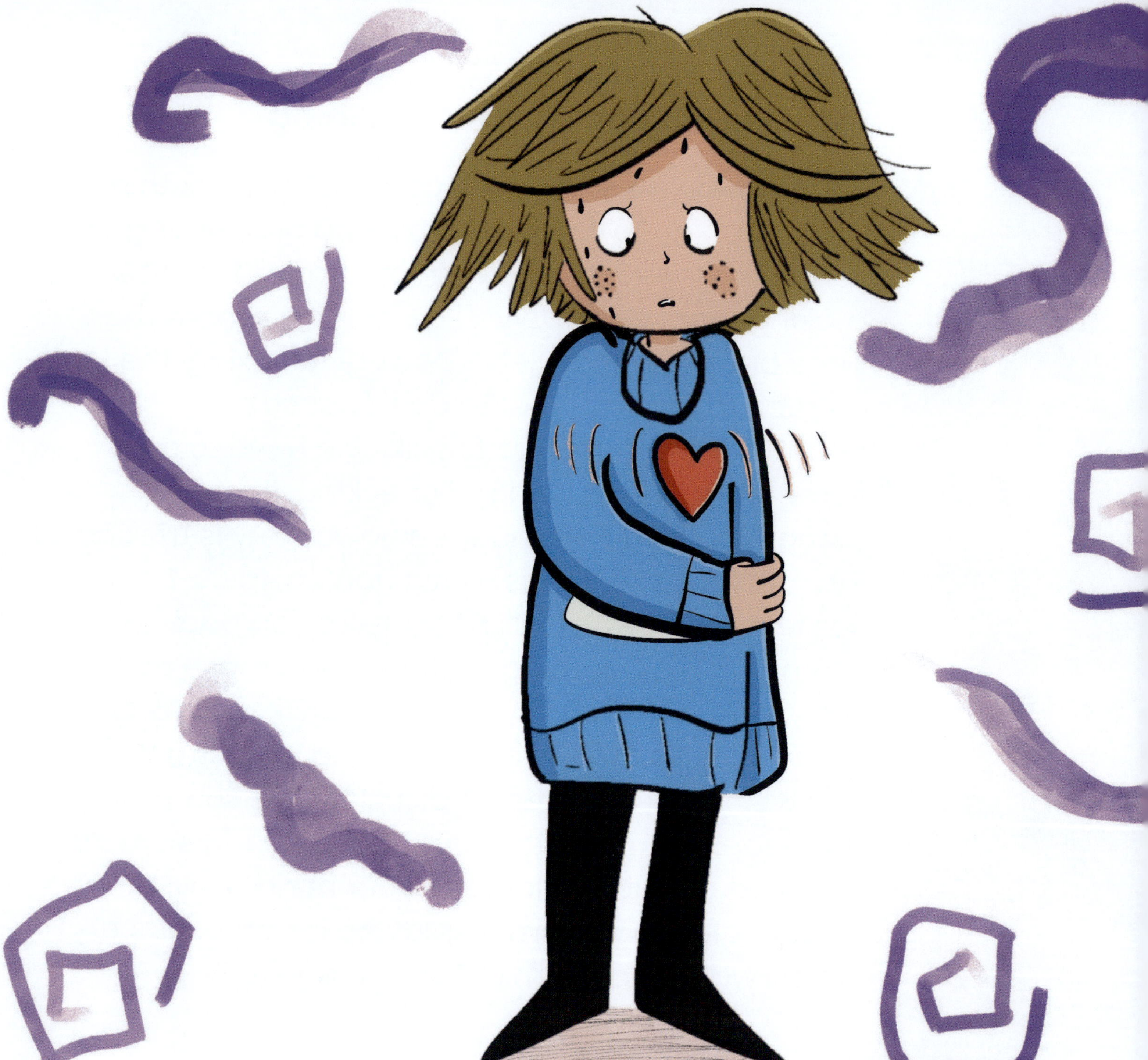

Panic

Sometimes we get anxious very quickly and we don't know why. We're not even aware of a thought we've had that might trigger anxiety. We start to panic and have a lot of anxiety symptoms especially a racing heart. We start to panic because the symptoms are so strong. We call it a panic attack.

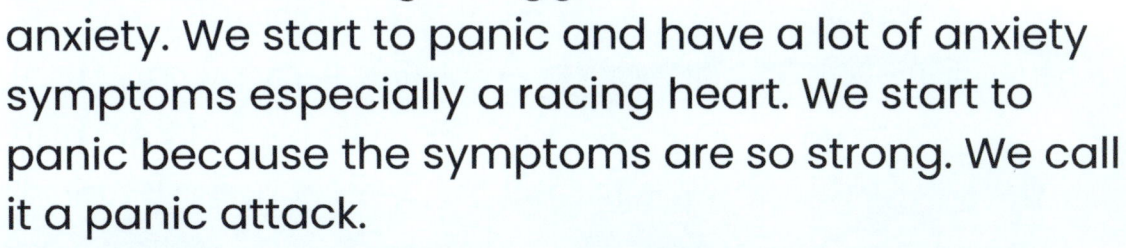

Panic attacks can be very frightening. You might think you're losing control, having a heart attack or even dying. This sudden and unexpected reaction means you're unprepared to deal with the anxiety, but now that you know that it is just anxiety…the caveman brain reaction that we all have…and now that you know how to calm yourself down by deep breathing…you'll be ready to deal with the panic you feel. Be brave, deep breathe and put anxiety in its place – well done! Just because it came on quickly, doesn't mean we can't deal with it – WE CAN!!

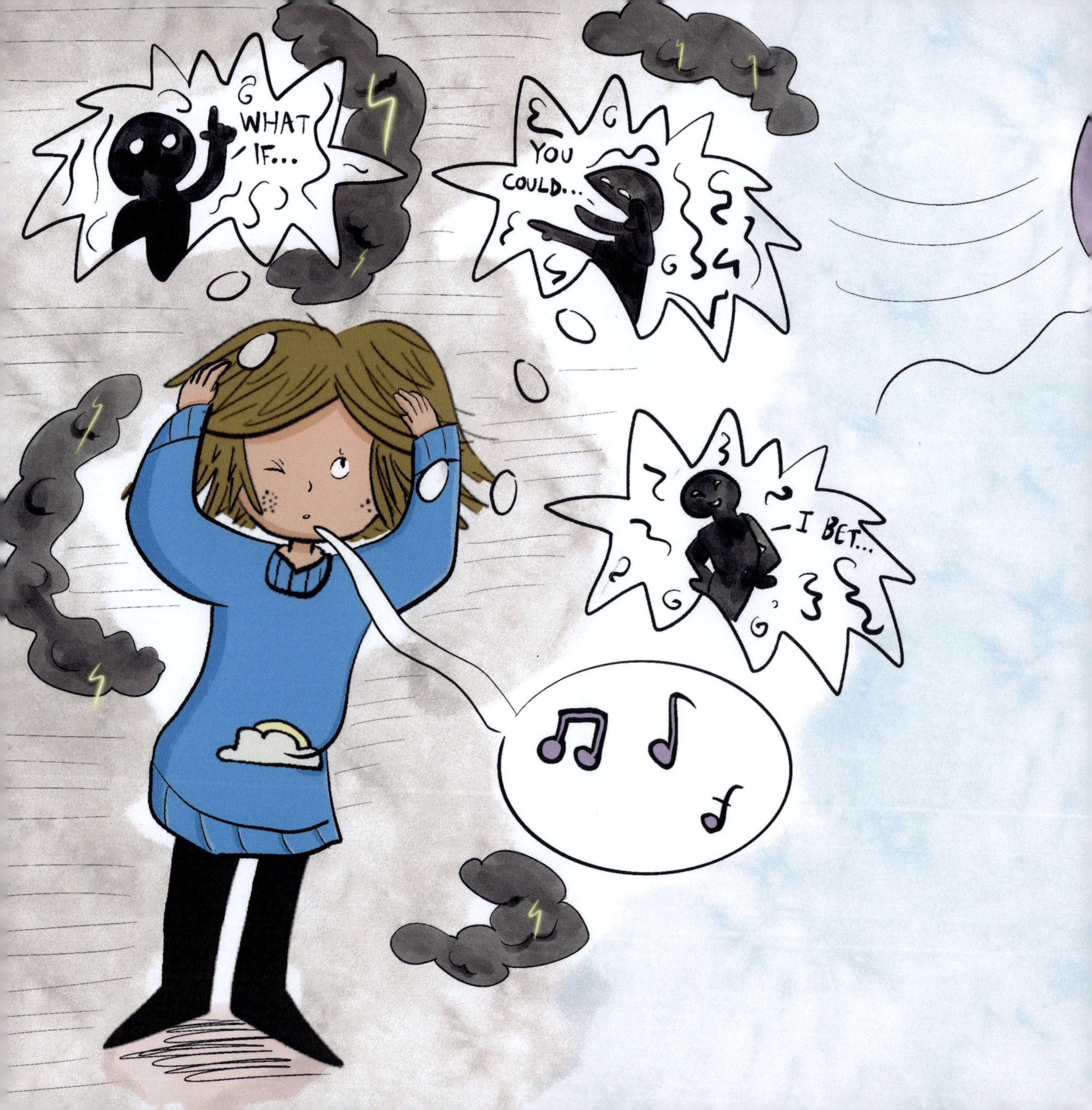
WHAT IF...
YOU COULD...
I BET...

Unwelcome thoughts

Sometimes we get thoughts that intrude. They are disruptive, annoying, unwelcome and uninvited. It's not helpful if we get these thoughts popping into our heads and upsetting us, stopping us from doing what we need to do. It doesn't make us a bad person if we get them. It's anxiety that is causing them and we need to let the thoughts go and not give them any importance. Perhaps you could do what I do: I sing a song that helps me to let these unwanted thoughts go! Concentrating on the words of the song helps me to forget about them. Don't forget to be brave and talk to a trusted adult about these thoughts, so they can help you to let them go, like a balloon released into the sky.

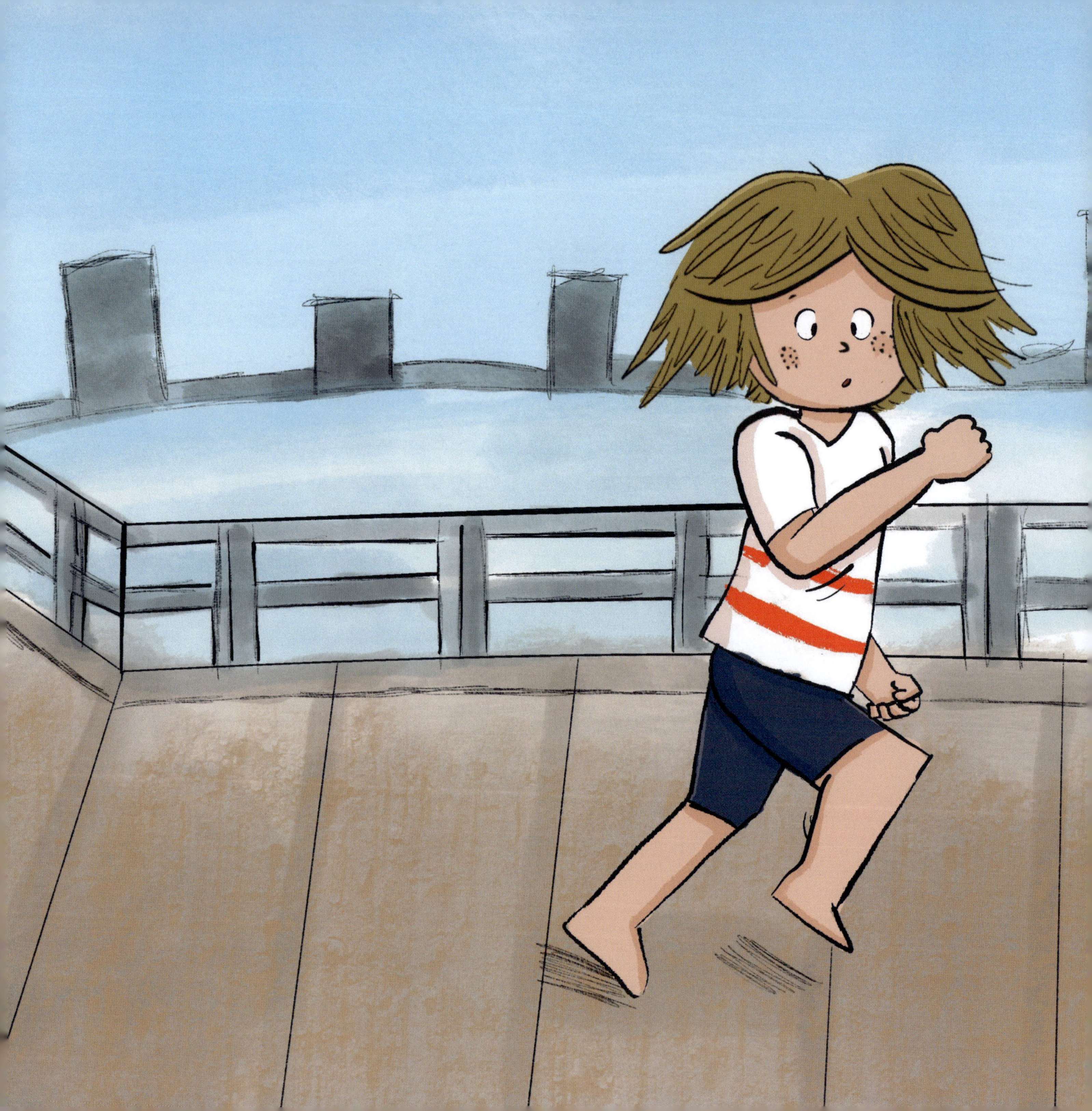

The importance of exercise

The main reason for the brain releasing adrenaline into the bloodstream is to give the body energy to deal with what it thinks is a danger or threat. Mostly there is no real danger and we don't need the energy to run away or to fight for something, so the adrenaline is not useful and it leaves our muscles feeling tight and sore. It is important to use up the energy by exercising. Ask your family what you can do to use up the energy. What about doing some trampolining, going on your family (dog) walk, doing some jumping jacks or running on the spot? This will help you to relax and sleep better and also stop aching muscles.

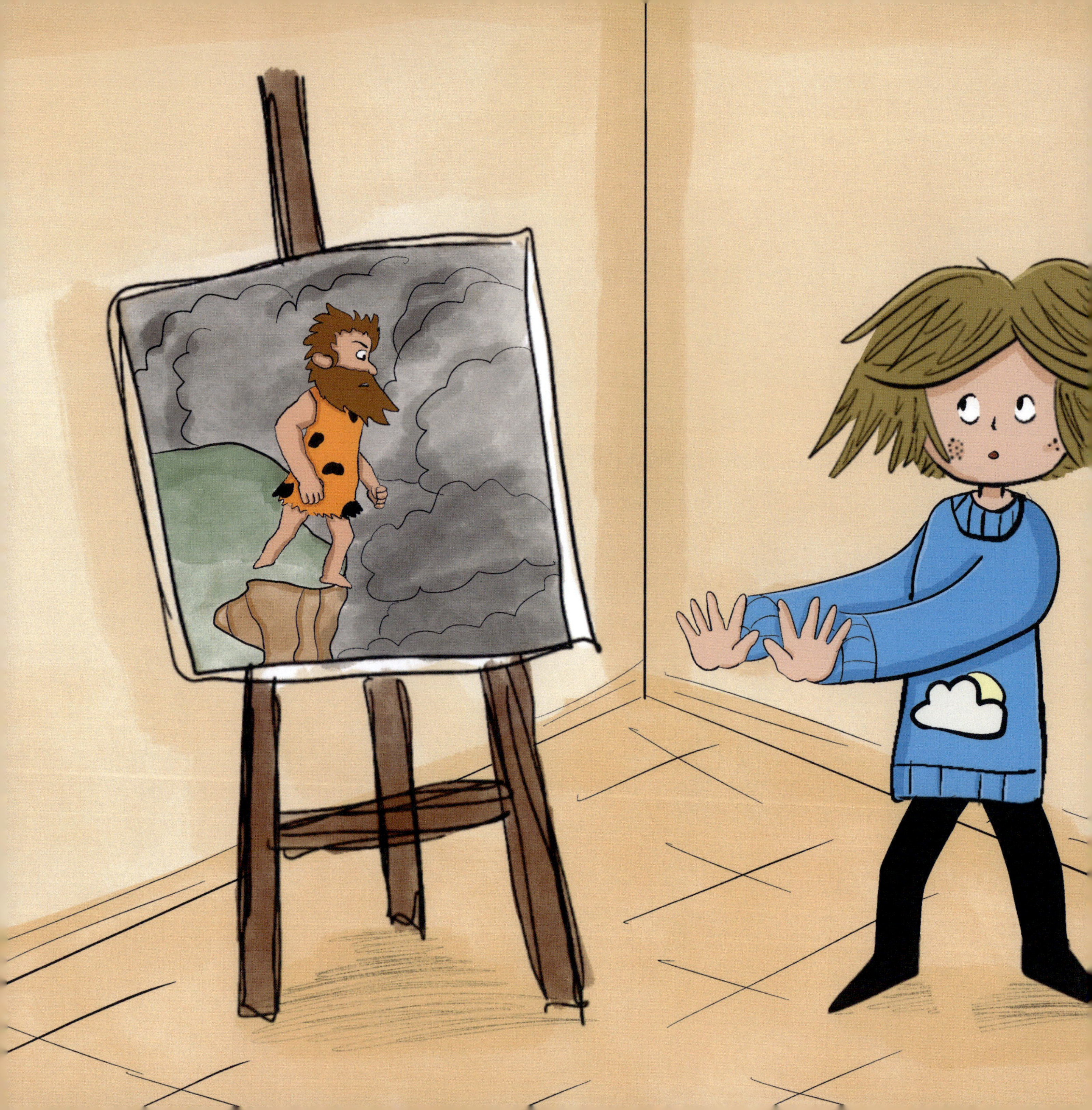

What does God say about anxiety?

Anxiety is part of our human nature; we all have anxiety. It is there for our safety. Humans would not have survived if they didn't have anxiety. They would have fallen off cliffs, got eaten by sabre-toothed tigers or fallen into deep water! Anxiety kept them safe from real dangers. God understands because he made us, and he wants us to learn to put anxiety in its place. He can also cope if we're angry about our anxiety being out of control and a problem. Let Him know if you're struggling with anxiety and ask for His help. At the end of this book is a prayer that I say when I'm struggling with anxiety. Perhaps you'd like to say it too.

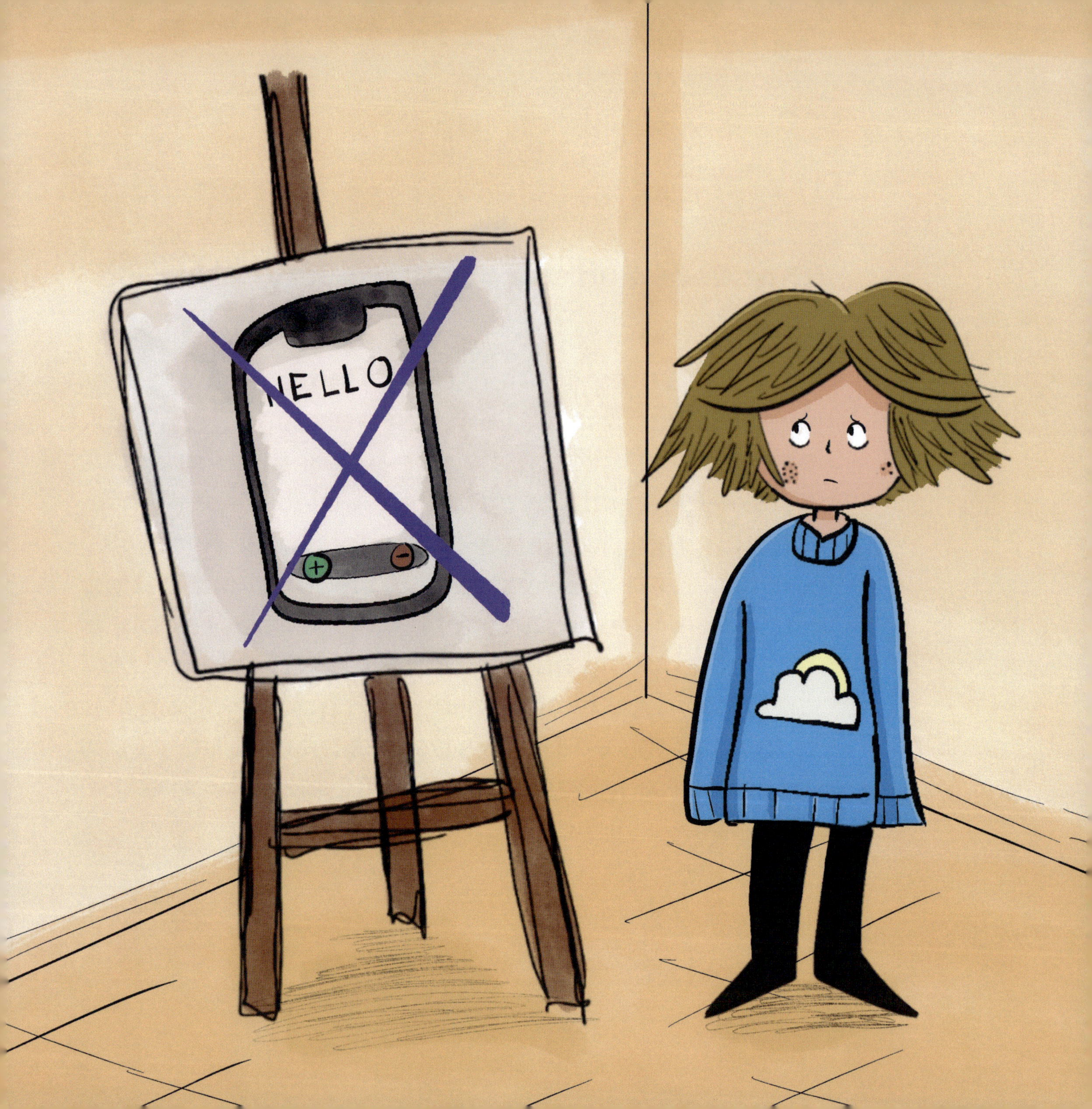
HELLO

Technology

Scientists have done research to see what effect using technology has on children's brains. They have found that spending too much time on phones, tablets or games consoles can make us feel sad and anxious. Ask your parents or carers to help you set a limit of what is acceptable for you. It is important to look after our mind and brain, as well as our bodies. Scientists have also discovered that it's important to stop using technology at least one hour before bedtime, because if we don't, it can stop us from falling asleep easily.

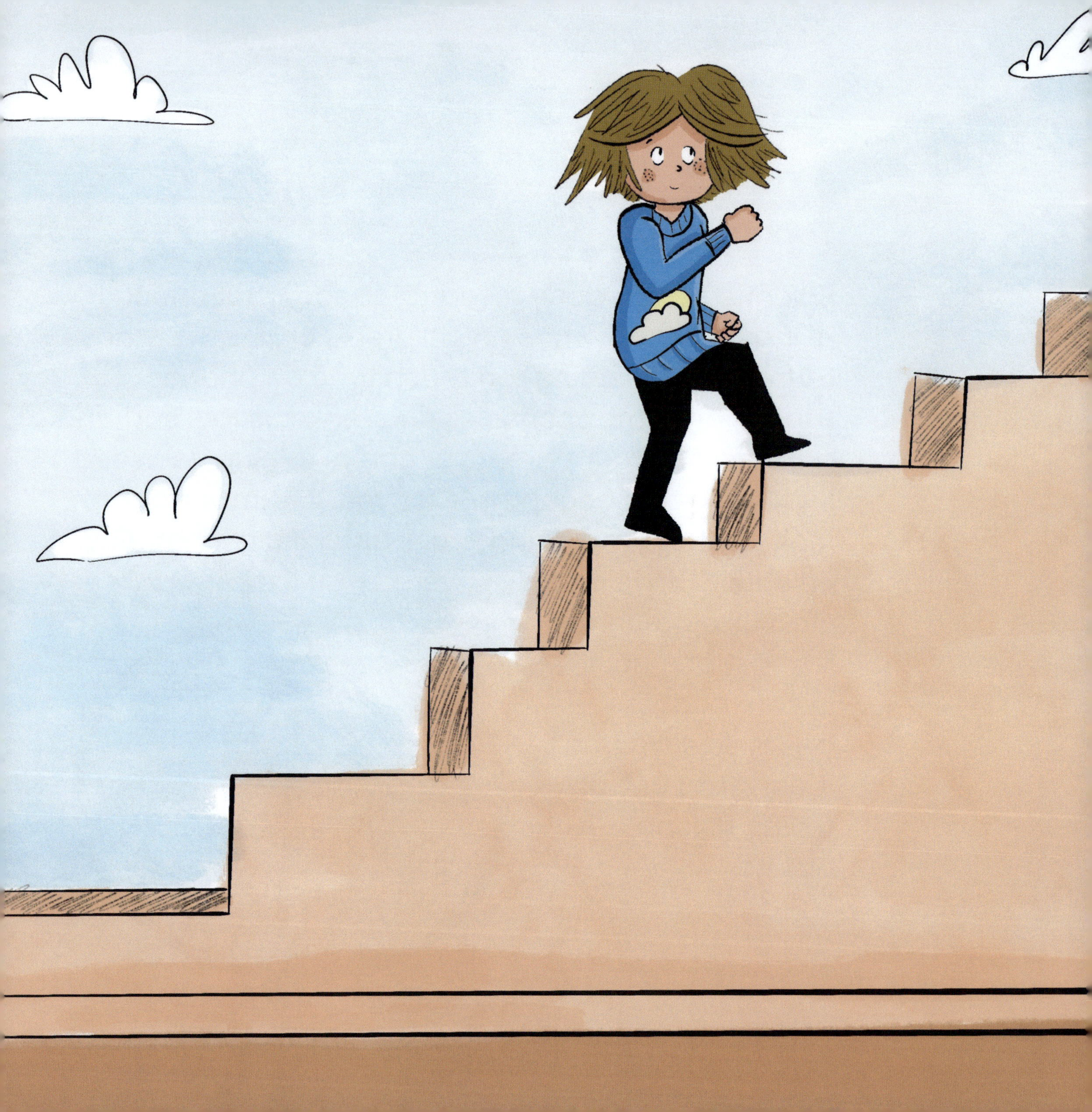

Little by little...gradually

When we're really worried about doing something, we need to do it little by little...very gradually...and not jump in at the 'deep end'; not try to do it all at once. What are you worried about: starting a new school, joining a club, reading out loud, singing a solo, going up in a lift, going to a friend's house or something else? Ask an adult to break it down into small steps that you can achieve or 'climb' one at a time.

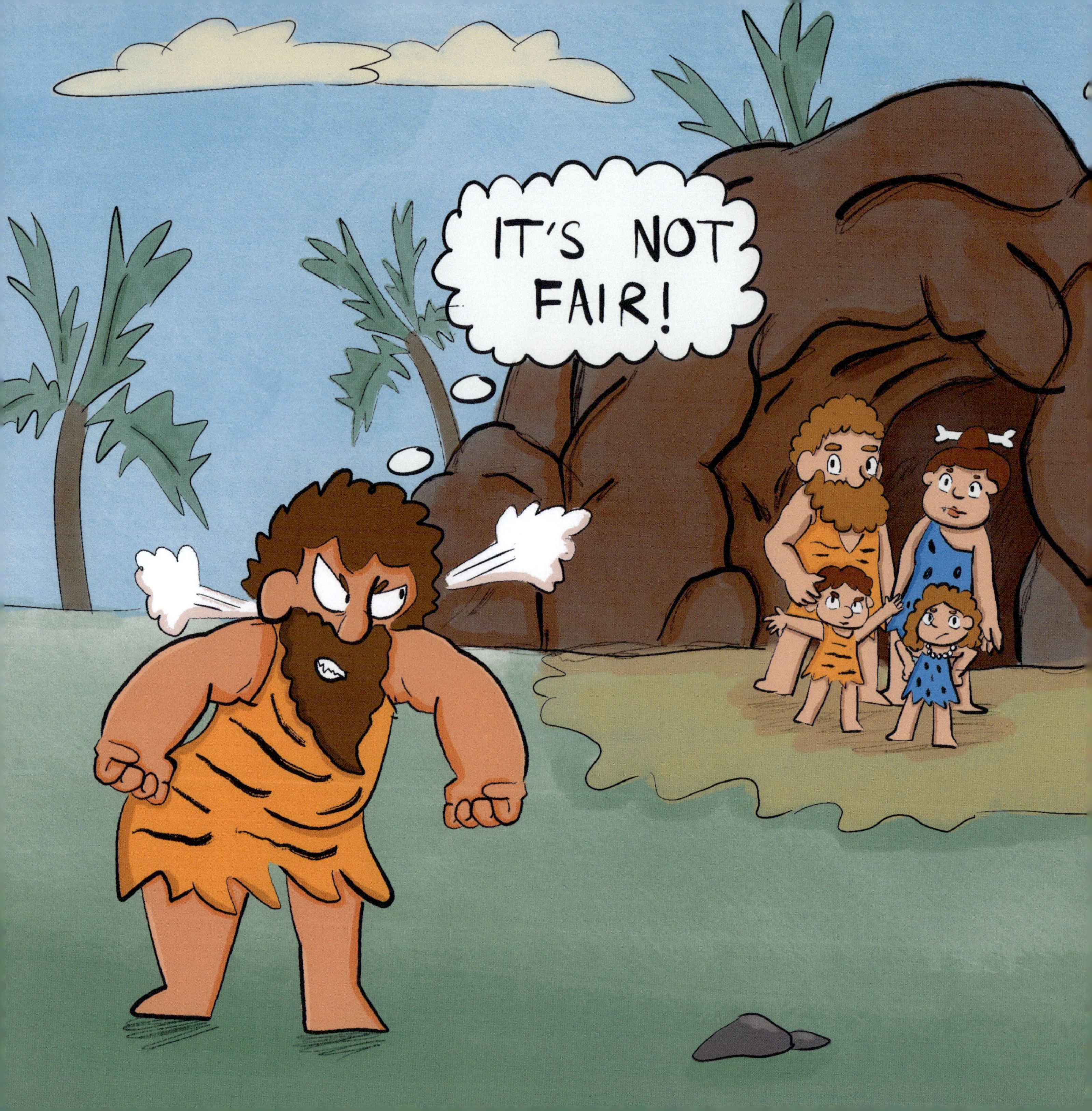
IT'S NOT FAIR!

So what about the fight...the anger?

So what about the **fight** in fight and flight?....the anger? What makes the alarm system go off this time? It's usually the thought that something is unfair. The same alarm system goes off with this thought, and the brain tells the body to prepare to fight (get angry). Imagine if you're a caveman who has been out hunting all day and you come home to find another cave family in your cave! You're going to get angry and want to fight for your cave back. Cave people couldn't reason, explain or discuss like we can so they fought to get back what was theirs. Remember that we have a voice and we CAN reason, explain or discuss. Our voice is an amazing tool and we can say, "I'm angry because ...(you've taken my cave) please...(give it back to me now)!" Once the alarm system has gone off, our heart will beat faster and we may get sweaty, red in the face, have tense muscles, and clenched fists.

It's ok to be angry, but it's not ok to ……….

More about anger

As with anxiety, we need to calm ourselves down so that the thinking part of our brain works and we can make better choices. Again, deep breathing helps. If I can remember to calm myself down before I say or do anything, I'm in control of my anger and I won't get myself into more trouble. It's ok to feel angry, but it isn't ok to hurt yourself, anyone else or anything, like objects or furniture. If we do any of these things, we will get ourselves into more trouble. If we don't calm ourselves down when we are angry, one thing leads to another. We are like a bull in a china shop causing lots of damage, or like a volcano exploding swear words, rudeness, thumping fists and kicking feet. To put anger in its place, we need to calm ourselves down. Deep breathing helps in the same way as it helps to put anxiety in its place. Counting to 10 before you say anything can help too, or counting backwards from 20 to zero.

We are happier humans when anxiety and anger are put in their place.

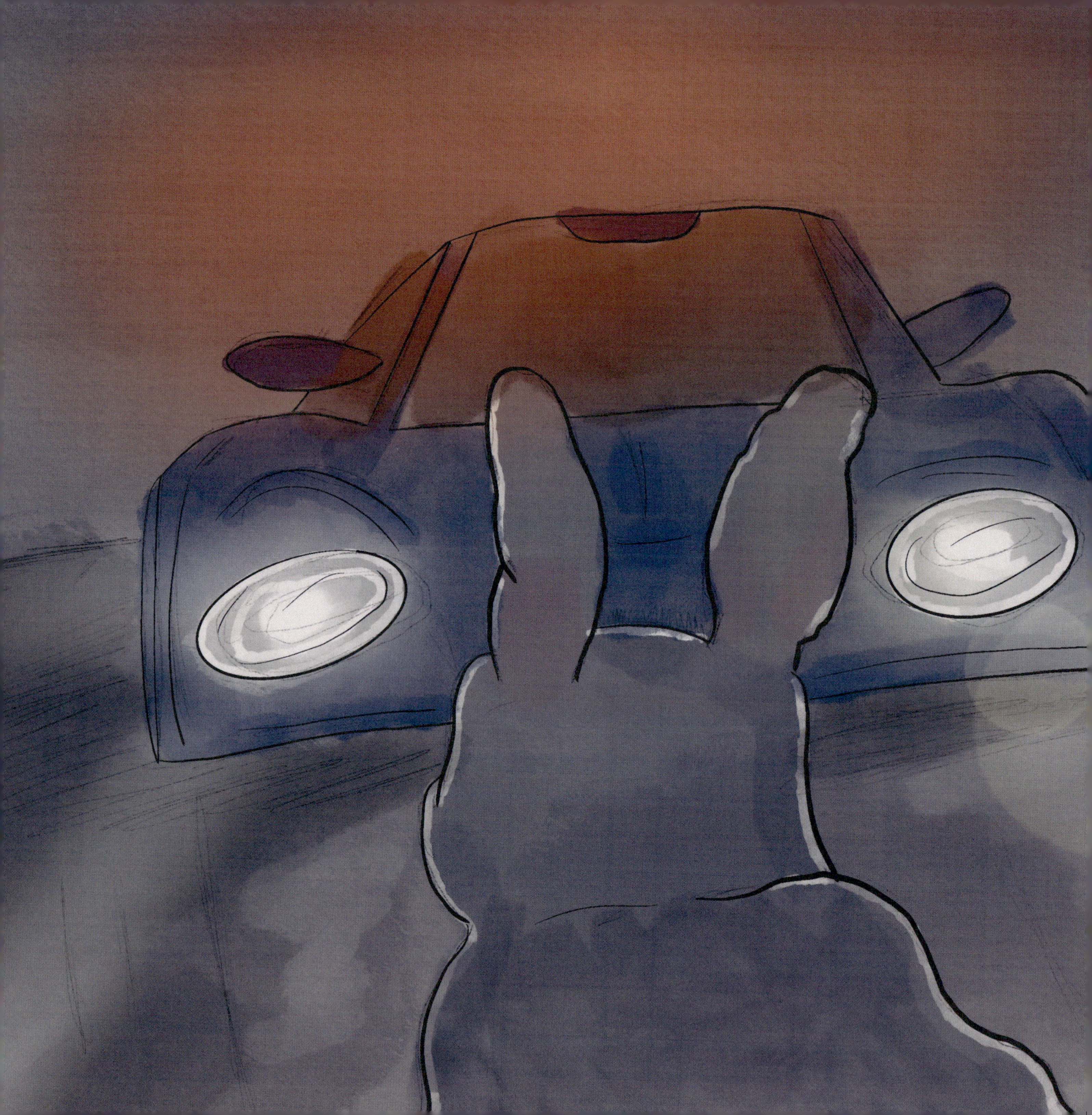

And finally...Freeze

One more thing...as well as fight and flight, there's also **freeze**...like a rabbit that gets scared when in the middle of the road, it's dark, and a car with bright headlights is coming towards it. The rabbit is so scared it freezes, and will get run over if it can't get its thinking brain working and move out of the way. You see when the alarm of fight, flight or freeze kicks in, it's the caveman or primitive part of the brain that is in control. When it happens to us, we feel like we can't speak or move. We need to get the new thinking part of our brain working by calming down and then we can make better choices. Can you remember how to calm down? Deep breaths and anything else that relaxes you.

Remember it's ok to get angry: it's normal but calm down and then say why you're angry. Your calm voice is your greatest tool in helping someone understand what you're angry about. You, like me, will feel better when you have kept anger in its place. We are stronger than our emotions!

Anxiety and anger are normal and we can learn to manage them and keep them in their place

Finally...I hope that I have helped you to see that anxiety and anger are normal, we all have them, and we are stronger than them both. We have learned lots of ways to put them in their proper place...where we can control them and they don't control us!

"Bye".

The End

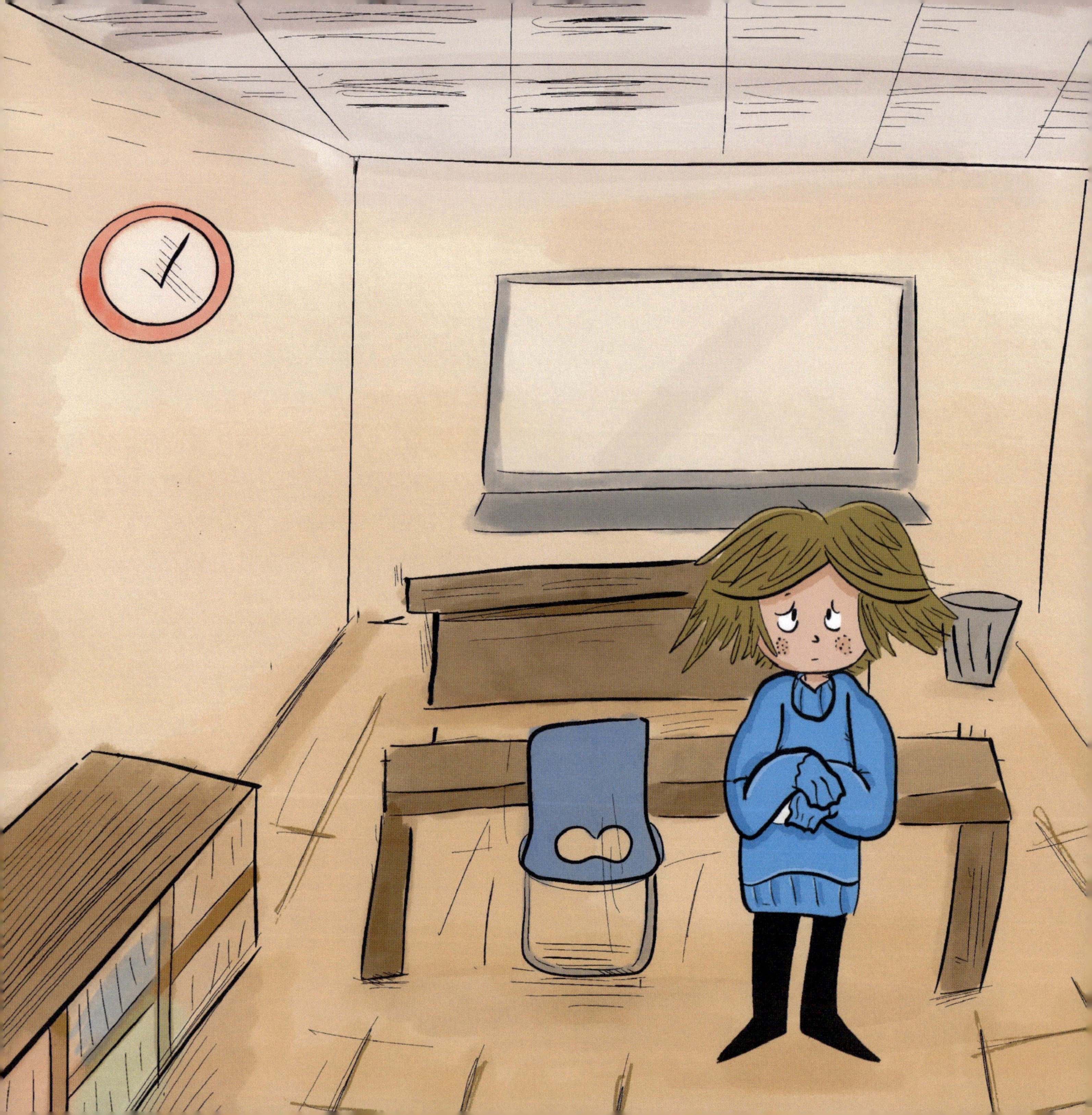

Appendix

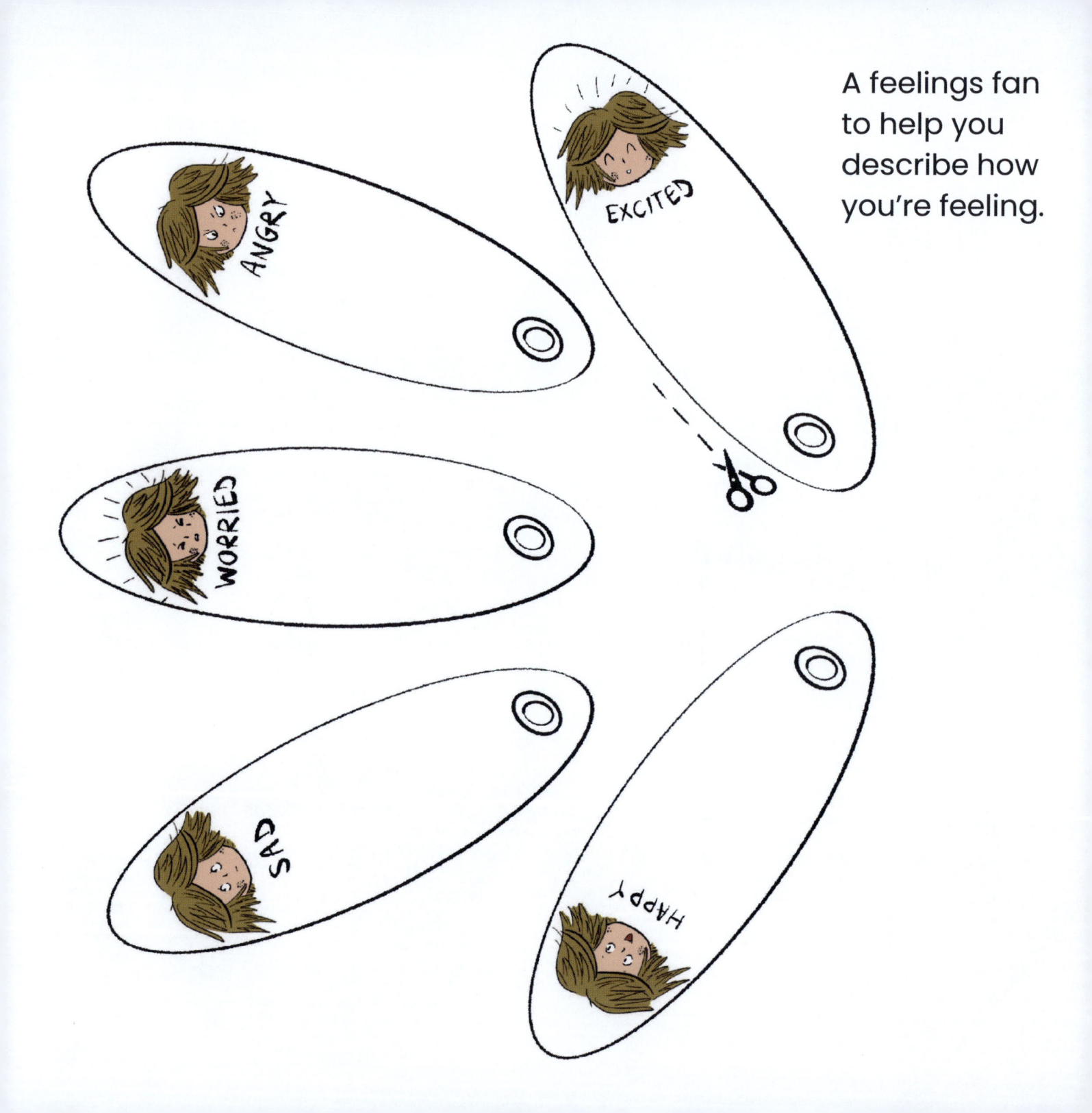

A feelings fan to help you describe how you're feeling.

Looking after our mind

Just like we look after our bodies, we need to look after our minds. We call this emotional health or mental health. Here is a checklist so that you can tick off each one:

Eat plenty of healthy food like fruit and vegetables

Do some exercise everyday

Drink lots of water

Primary school children need between 9 and 12 hours sleep every night

Do some relaxation for a few minutes everyday like mindfulness

Talk to a trusted adult about anything that is bothering you

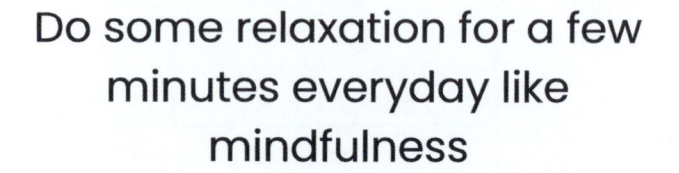

Practise deep breathing when you know you're anxious

Help other people whenever you can: it makes you feel good about yourself

Find something you like doing eg a sport or a craft and get as good as you can at it. This will make you feel good about yourself too

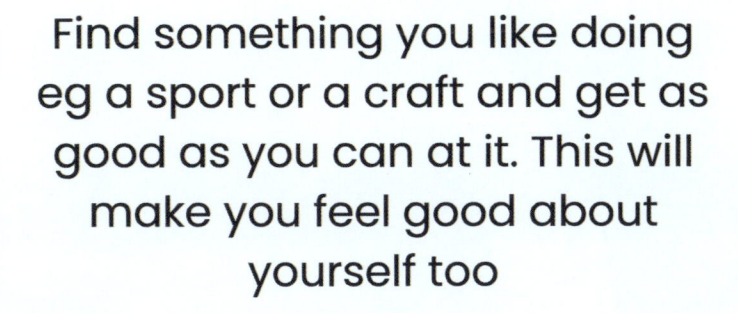

Don't spend too long on technology (phone, tablet or games console) as it can make you feel sad and anxious.

63

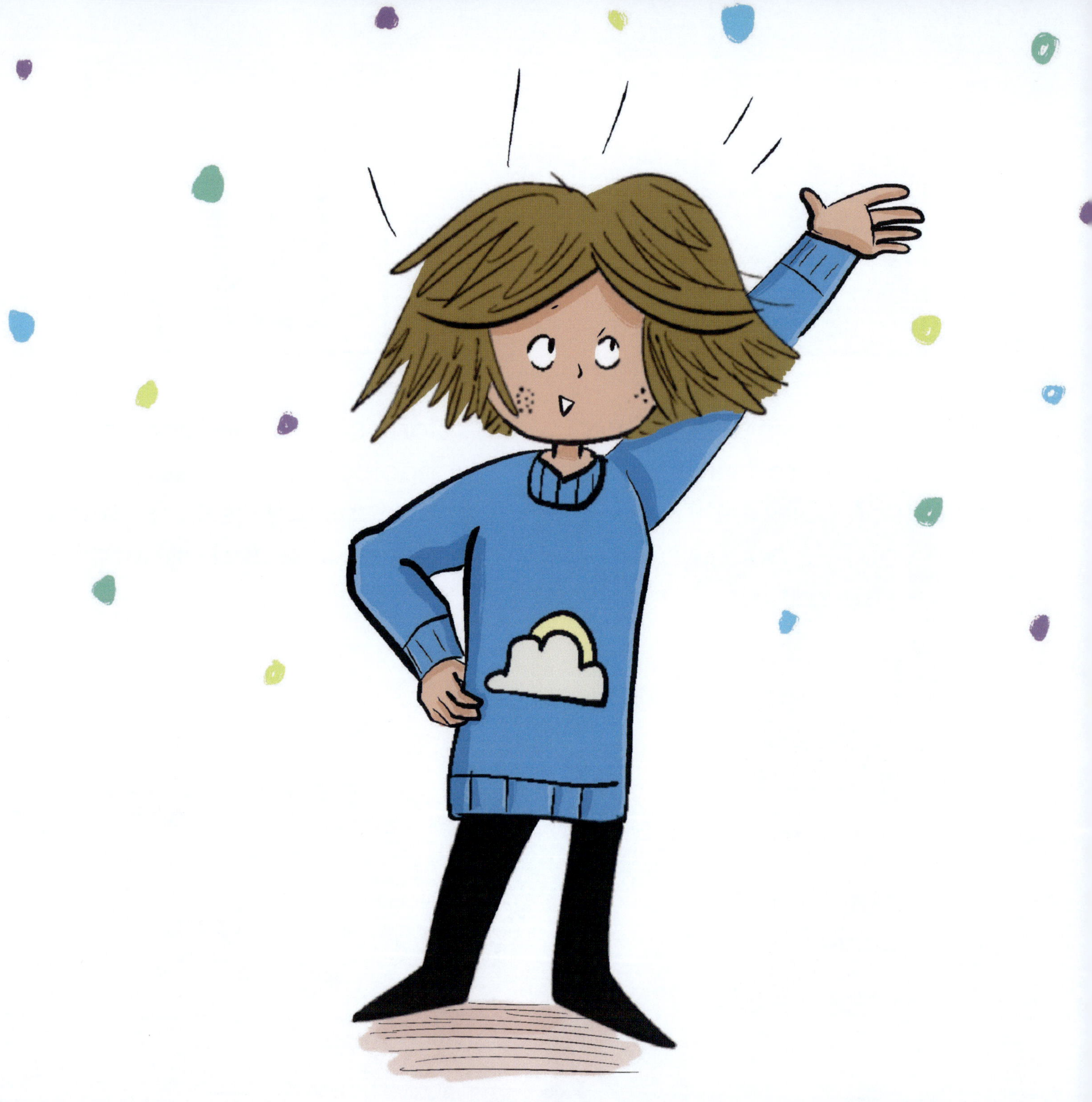

Dear God

I'm angry that I have anxiety! Why? I know that it is part of your design to keep the human race going, and useful for the energy to run a race or to sit a test. It also ensures that I complete my homework and do the things I'm asked to do, but why does it make me feel so bad and stop me from doing the things I want to do? Why do I feel the need to do unhelpful things to make the anxiety go away? I'm told that sometimes anxiety gets out of control and needs managing. Please help me to be the boss of my anxiety and to control it in helpful ways, rather than it controlling me! I pray that you will help me to restore my anxiety to the level that you intended it to be; for example to run a race and to keep me safe around water and traffic. God, please help me to be brave enough to talk about my anxiety with those I trust and also help me to be brave and face my fears. Help me to find ways to cope that will help me whenever I need them. Please help me to appreciate that anxious people are the most conscientious and achieve well in life because of this: help me to be proud of myself and who I am. When anxiety is put in its place, I will be happy again.

Thank you God

Amen

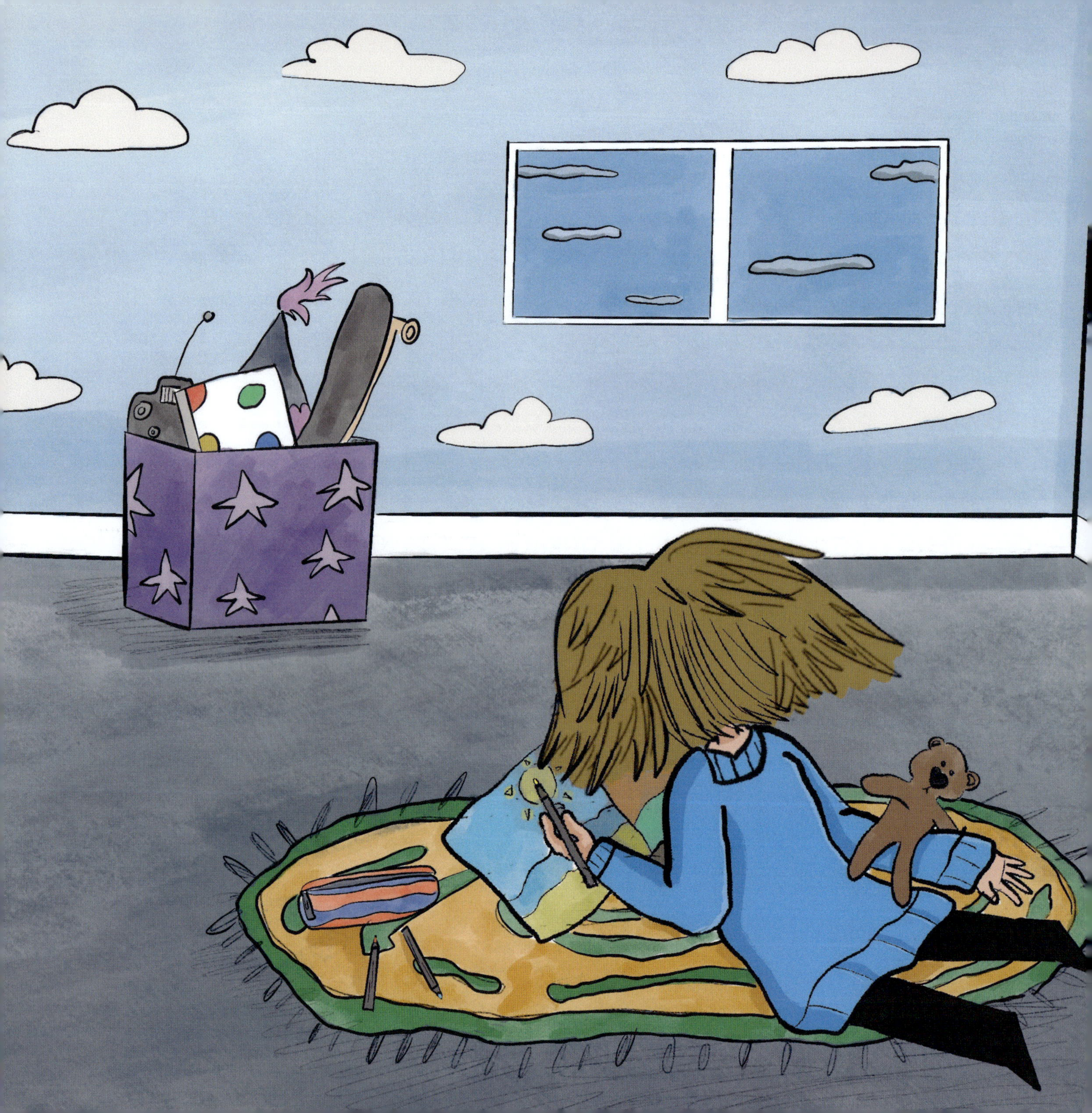

A pretend 'journey' to go on to help you relax

Ask an adult to read this to you once you have tensed and relaxed all your muscles from top to toe and done some deep breaths.

Get comfortable in a chair. Close your eyes. Think about your bottom and back touching the chair and your feet on the floor. Listen to the sounds you can hear in the room, and then outside the room you're in.

Now you're ready to go on an imaginary adventure.

Imagine there is a little door in the room that you can squeeze through into a lovely field full of long grass and wild flowers. The sun is shining and its warm. You can smell the scent of the flowers. Feel the long grass with your hands. You can hear the sea as you approach the sand dunes. Take off your shoes and socks and feel the warm sand under your feet. Are you ready to paddle in the sea? Can you feel the cool water lapping over your toes? You see the rock pools and head for them, letting the warm seawater splash up your legs as you walk along. You find a large rock pool to sit by and there you see tiny fishes darting between the seaweed and a miniature crab hiding in the sand. Starfishes and sea anemones add colour and interest to the pool...When you've tired of looking in the rock pool and the sun is beginning to lose its warmth, you set off home, enjoying the sand under your feet again. Wash your feet under the cold water tap as you leave the beach. Dry your feet with your fluffy towel and put your shoes and socks back on. Notice how relaxed your feet feel. Head for the field of long grass and wild flowers. Again let the long grass slip through your fingers and look for the tiny doorway back into the room. Squeeze through and sit in your chair. Listen for the sounds both outside and then inside the room. Be aware of your feet on the floor and your back and bottom against the chair. If you're doing this to help you sleep, keep your eyes shut and continue your imaginary journey to somewhere you feel happy and safe. Your imagination can take you anywhere you want.

If you have done this journey to help you relax in the daytime, open your eyes when you are ready. You should now feel relaxed and ready to do whatever it is that you need to do.

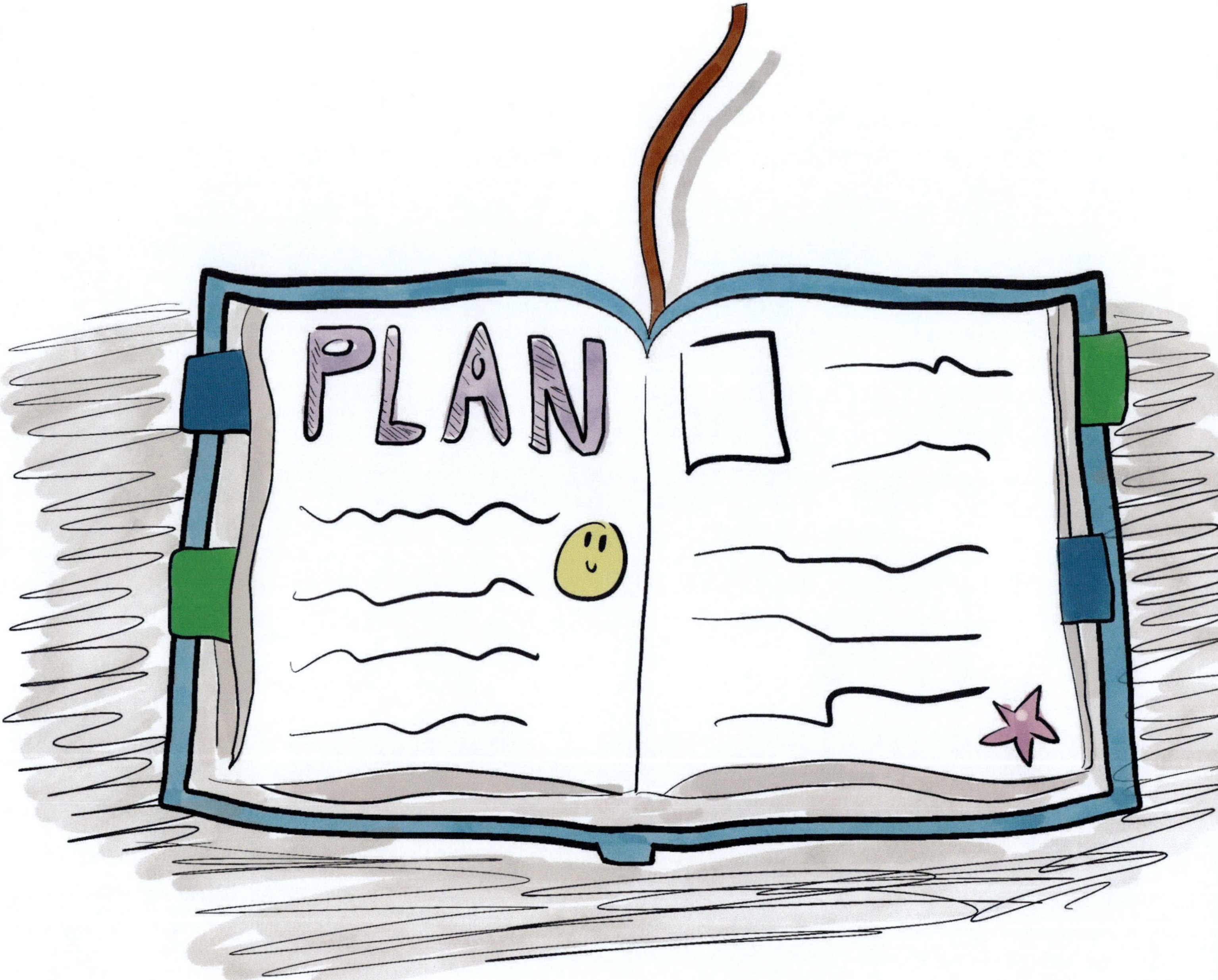
PLAN

About this book

This book is written for 7 to 12 year olds, to help them understand what happens in their body when they get anxious and what they can do to help their bodies go back to normal as quickly as possible and achieve what they need to achieve. It is written to explain anxiety on a simple level, from experience of what works with this age group. It may not be completely accurate from a medical or scientific point of view but this can be learned at a later stage in life. The author has taken a wholistic approach to tackling anxiety from a physical, emotional and spiritual point of view. She has based the book around problems that primary school children have raised with her.

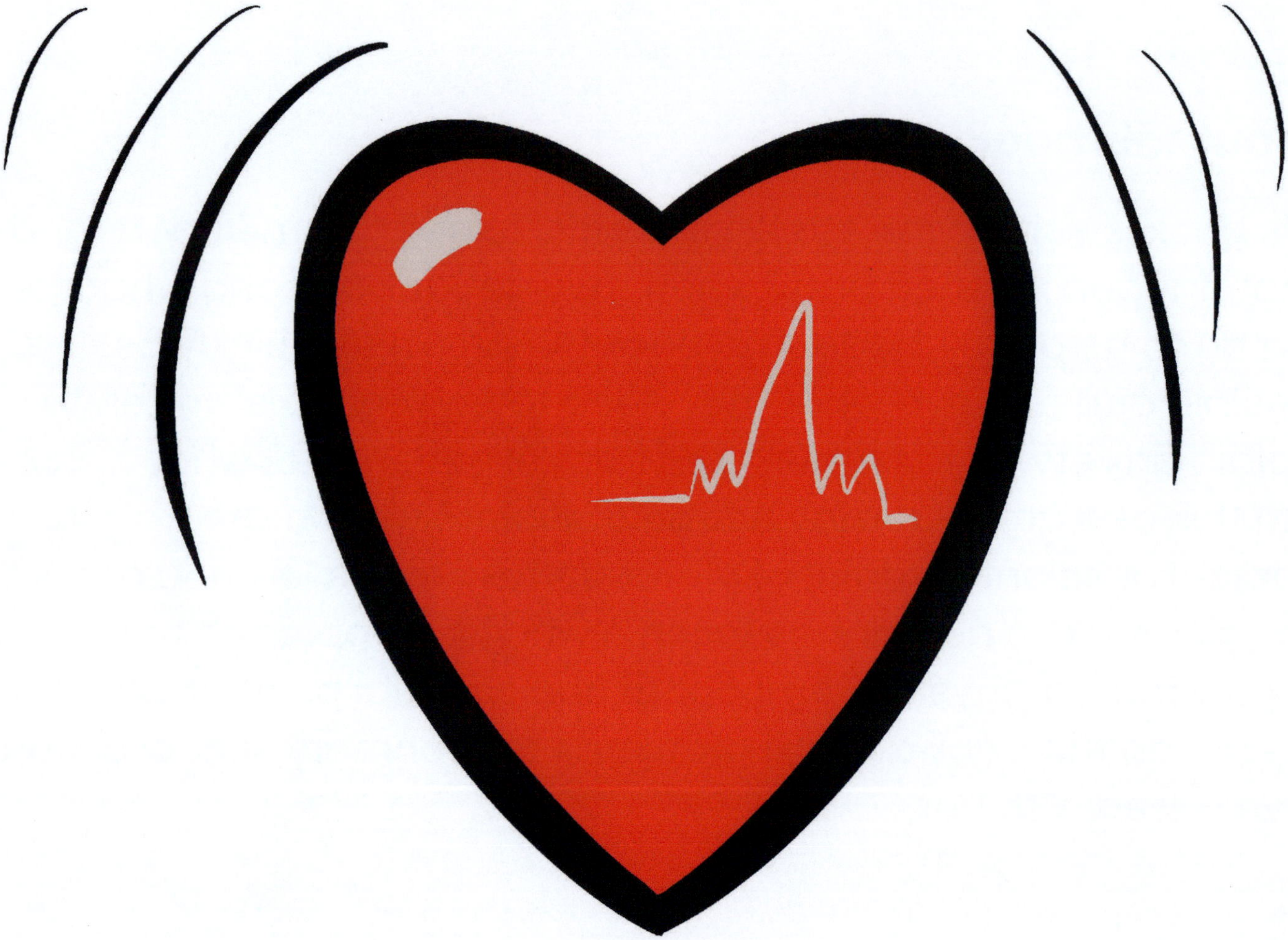

About the author

Sally trained as a primary school teacher in the mid to late 1980s at Manchester Polytechnic, Didsbury School of Education and has worked largely in Nottinghamshire primary schools. In 2004 she started to train as a counsellor at Nottingham Trent University and after qualifying did some training with Place2Be to work largely with primary school children. She is currently working in Nottinghamshire with children who are struggling in mainstream primary schools, for a variety of reasons, including anxiety.

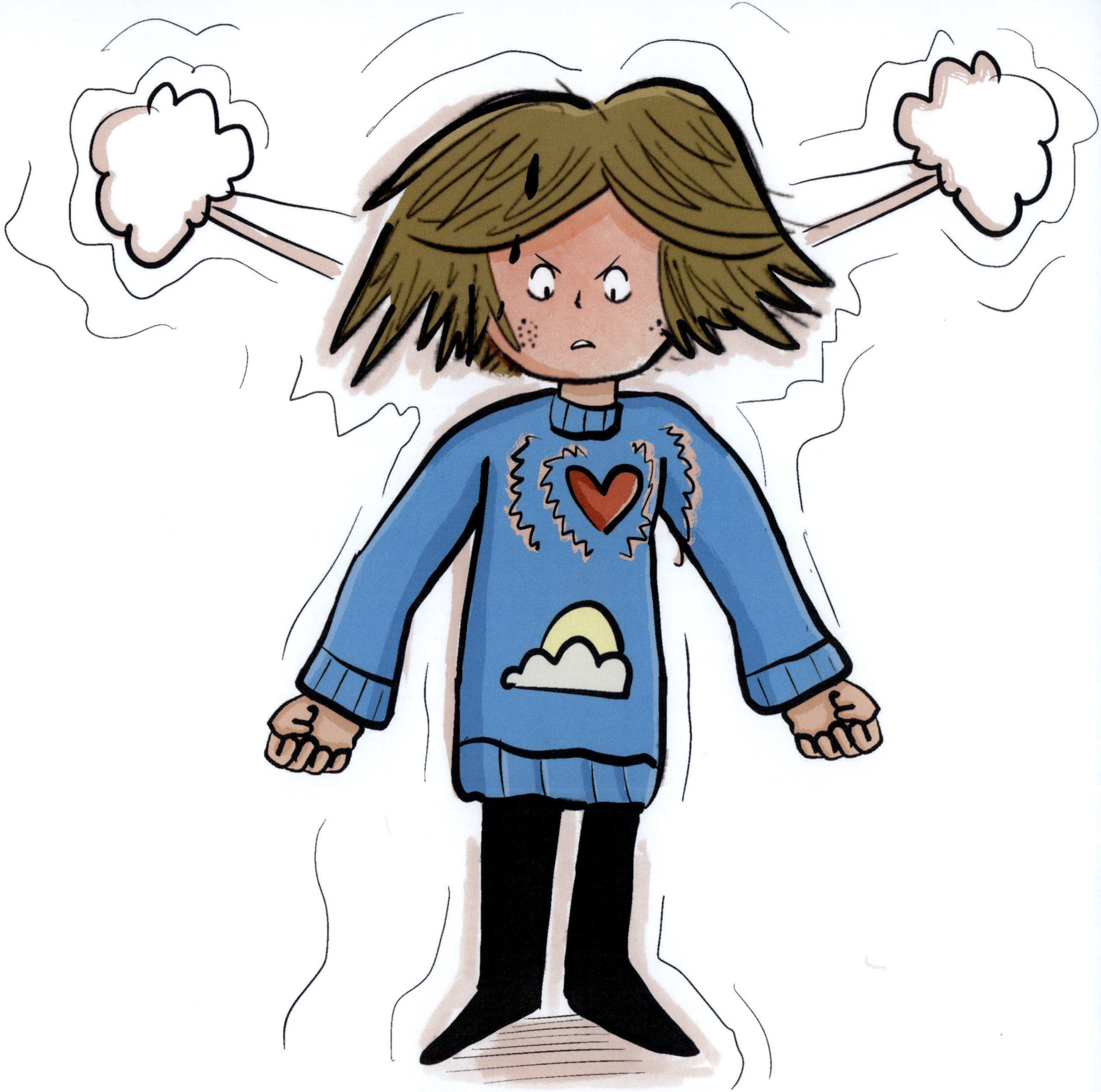

Index

Anger	7, 51, 53, 55	God	45, 65
Avoiding	19	Hand washing	37
Bedtime	27	Mindfulness	25
Counting	37	Nature	25
Deep breathing	13, 53	Prayer	65
Exercise	43	Relaxation	27, 67, 68, 69
Fight and flight	7, 9, 11, 29	Technology	47, 63
Five finger breathing	15	Talking	23, 33
Freeze	55	Unwelcome thoughts	41